CONTENT MARKE

DISCLAIM

CW01668547

The information presented in this report solely and fully represents the views of the author as of the date of publication. Any omission, or potential misrepresentation of, any peoples or companies is entirely unintentional. As a result of changing information, conditions or contexts, this author reserves the right to alter content at their sole discretion impunity.

The book is for informational purposes only and while every attempt has been made to verify the information contained herein, the author assumes no responsibility for errors, inaccuracies, and omissions. Each person has unique needs and this book cannot take these individual differences into account.

TABLE OF CONTENTS

INTRODUCTION

Content Marketing means creating and sharing content of high standards and shareable values to attract an audience for your digital empire. The primary objective of content marketing is to convert the prospects into customers and the customers into repeated buyers. Moreover, the type of content we create and share tells about our niche. Therefore, it can be termed as a strategic approach for creating and sharing content in such a manner which will set up and retain a clearly defined audience which will ultimately drive traffic and profitable customers.

Nowadays the smart marketers are using "Content Marketing" as the next big thing. There is no doubt about the fact that content marketing is an awesome medium to present yourself in the market and reach out to the audiences. Moreover, these days customers have given a set back to the traditional ways of marketing, this change in the mindset of customers has enhanced the role of content in marketing even more.

The best thing about content marketing is that it is non-interrupting marketing. It is not direct selling of products and services, instead of pitching them directly, you deliver information about your products and services that make our prospect a more intelligent choice. The main essence of this whole strategy lies in the one simple fact that if as businesses and service providers, we deliver consistent and ongoing valuable information to buyers.

In this book, we will talk about some essential steps to successful content marketing.

Let's begin!!!

CONTENT MARKETING

Content Marketing is a strategic marketing approach focused on creating and distributing valuable, relevant, and consistent content to attract and retain a clearly-defined audience and ultimately to drive profitable customer action. Content can be in the form of articles, videos, newsletters, podcasts and more. Ideally, you should stick to marketing one or two types of content until you see consistent results with them.

With content gaining high importance in today's world, several trends keep on coming up in the material world. Trending elements thus constitute a major part of successful content development. Following these trends, not only help with the content development but with its marketing too!

However, doing content marketing is not an easy task. The marketers present all over the net are finding it difficult to create content because the competition has become very tough. Everybody else is looking for creating unique content every day. So, it becomes very important to make sure that you can create such content to be in the game.

"Content Marketing is a commitment, not a campaign."

-Jon Buscall

It is the obvious fact that great content is a must for your content marketing. Content forms the base to drive inbound traffic and leads. Moreover, you need good and unique content for your PPC to work. But still, there are few present day problems related to content marketing which has made it difficult for the content marketers to make worthy content for marketing.

Let's have a look at the problem:

- The attention spans have become critically short
- The competitors in the digital market are now creating a very high volume of content with higher production value. Moreover, increased the cost to create competitive content people will deem worthy of their attention.

- **Insufficient Resources**

It is a fact that simply producing content is easier than producing a really high-quality content. Creating high-quality content means hiring qualified writers. For small businesses, content writing is an uphill job to do in house but outsourcing your content writing makes it more achievable, and you can inspect the marketing efforts without much hassle.

- **Changing Trends and Paid Promotion**

The content landscape is transforming at a quick pace. Most companies are resorting to paid promotion as much as they can. Though different platforms exist for the publicity and promotion, the emergence of social media platforms such as Twitter, Facebook, Google+, Tumblr and LinkedIn attract a lot of business owners, and they adhere to them. All these platforms provide advanced means to segment readers and to reach the targeted type of groups at the affordable price.

"Make it simple. Make it memorable. Make it inviting to look at. Make it fun to read."

Leo Burnett

But in order to produce a great content consistently, many factors or issues are to be addressed. One issue is time, and it becomes a big barrier in content marketing. Secondly, there is an issue of budget and many big businesses lack sufficient budget to hire a professional writer or team of writers in order to produce unique and excellent content for marketing purposes

What can be done about it?

Competition in the market has raised the bar in the digital market, and you can fight the above two problems in the following ways:

Start creating content at equal production value as that of your competitor, but make sure that you do it on more prestigious and trusted brand platforms. The advantage of such platform is that they have built-in audiences. This will bring trust and prestige to you and your content surely.

"You need to create ridiculously good content – content that is useful, enjoyable and inspired."

-Ann Handley

The second thing, which can be done is increasing the production value close to what your competitor has. Now, while doing this make sure that the usefulness and relevancy of your content should be much more than your competitors.

Both of the ways have the potential to solve the problems related to content marketing, but the second one should be more feasible as it does not take more investments regarding money. Either way, you choose they key to good content marketing is the way you promote your content. It simply follows the 80-20 rule, 20% of the work is writing good content, and the remaining 80% is your promotion.

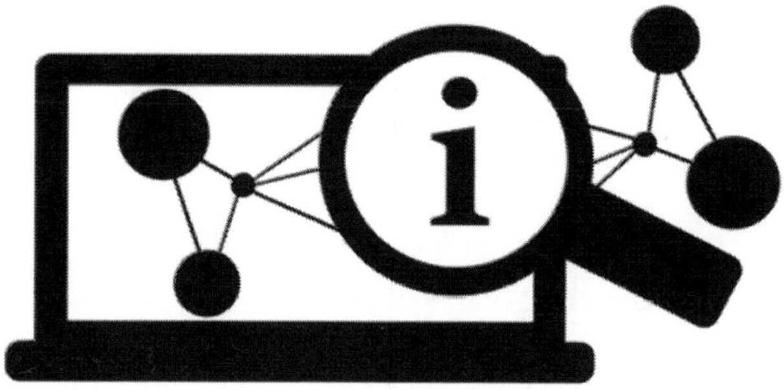

So, it must be now clear to you that content marketing has become the next big thing, but at the same time, it is not just a cake walk. Therefore, whether to choose it or not is totally your call.

How to Succeed With Content Marketing

Here are 6 stages to marketing your content successfully:

Stage 1

Know the purpose of producing a particular piece of content. Do you want to build up your brand as a business? Do you want to gain leads and subscribers? Do you want to make sales? Or do you want to connect with people? Knowing the purpose of your content means that you know the desired outcome, and you will produce the content in such a way that will give you that outcome.

Stage 2

Identify who you are speaking to with your content.

Who are you targeting?

Where do they hang out?

What do they want?

How can you provide a solution to them? Finding out the answers to these questions is essential to attract the right type of people to your content. Then you can produce relevant content that people are actually interested in and resonate with.

Stage 3

Plan your content. Planning and researching what you are going to write for your content is very useful if you want to produce quality and engaging content. What I like to do when planning my articles, is to search similar content on Google so that I can understand the similarities and differences when writing my articles.

Stage 4

Provide a Call to Action (CTA). In marketing, CTA is an instruction to the audience to provoke an immediate response that is usually given at the end of a piece of content. Including a call to action in your content will make sure that the reader is not left with anything at the end of the content, and instead, they can proceed with a follow-up action, which is related to the purpose of your content.

Stage 5

Market your Content. Producing quality content is one thing, but marketing it and getting people to notice it is another thing. There are many different ways of marketing your content. One way is to use Search Engine Optimisation (SEO). SEO is used to improve your rank in the search engine results such as Google. Including specific keywords in your content will help you rank better in the search engines when people search those keywords. Other ways of marketing your content include Social Media, Email Marketing, Pay-per-click (PPC) and Paid Ads.

Stage 6

Evaluate your Content. The final stage is to evaluate your content to understand which content is producing results and which isn't. From there you can apply more of what works, and less of what doesn't work.

"Content is king, but distribution is queen. And she wears the pants."

- Jonathan Perelman

Make sure that you grasp these 6 stages to ensure that you Succeed With Content Marketing:

1. Know the Purpose of the Content

2. Identify your Audience

3. Plan your Content

4. Provide a Call to Action

5. Market your Content

6. Evaluate your Content

Why Do We Create Content At All?

Why is quality content important for you to stand out as a consultant selling productized services?

Your best client expects to see content

The reality is that clients expect to be able to go online and search your company no matter what you sell. Your BEST client expects to go to a search engine, type in your niche (or website name), and find something about your business

It's the content that differentiates

So when prospective clients search for your company what content do they find? Will they find compelling, sharp content that sparks their interest to learn more about your company? Or will they find random, disconnected articles you wrote 3 years ago and forgot all about? Your BEST client is going to use what they find to decide if they want to engage with your business...and this happens way before a phone call or another inquiry is ever placed.

You want the prospective client prepared before you talk

Your free consultation should not be a 45-minute call where you explain your entire menu of services to a half-interested, half-overwhelmed prospective client. It should be more like a 15-minute call where they acknowledge that they "like what they've seen" and want to discuss a relationship going forward. Best case scenario, you don't want to bid or compete for a client. It should be abundantly clear that you are the BEST solution to their problem.

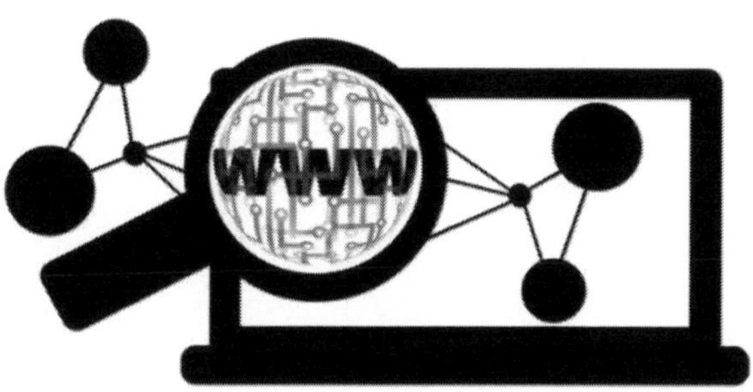

The 6 Flavors of Content Marketing

It's important to understand what type of content marketer you are. Make sure you establish this before you move forward and document your plan.

1. **Brand Builder:** If your flavour is a brand builder, kudos. Capture readers with entertaining, educational pieces of content that incorporate brand messaging, and they will perceive your brand as trustworthy, credible, and likeable.

2. **Thought Leader:** The thought leader knows that there is little that can match content marketing's effectiveness in terms of making owners, principals or executives appear as the people who set the agenda for the industry

3. **Lead Nurturer:** You have more leads than you know what to do with — and not enough competent sales people to stay on top of them. Get your CRM lead data cleaned up, fire up your marketing automation tool, and start dropping smart content in your prospects' laps.
4. **Social Media Manager:** You're the hit-or-miss flavour. Social media activity should be only one part of a strong content marketing plan — don't let

the social media tail wag the content marketing dog.

5. **Lead Generator:** While content marketing will generate short-term leads, those leads are not necessarily "sales-ready." Make content marketing the supporting cast to your existing or new programs.

6. **Publicity Seeker:** Otherwise known as the "Replace PR with Content Marketing, Expect Same Benefits" approach, this flavour is almost always a poor choice. Content marketing contributes to but does not create media coverage.

"The best marketing doesn't feel like marketing."

- Tom Fishburne

THE BENEFITS OF CONTENT MARKETING

Traditionally, marketers have had to rent (or beg) attention from other people's media – through display ads on websites, booths at a tradeshow, or emails sent to third-party lists. In short, companies have essentially "rented" attention that someone else built. For example, when a brand pays out millions of dollars for a Super Bowl ad., they are "renting" attention that the TV networks have built.

"Stop writing about everything. So many brands create content and try to cover everything, instead of focusing on the core niche that they can position themselves as an expert around. No one cares about your special recipe... Find your niche, and then go even more niche."

Joe Pulizzi

Content marketing, on the other hand, allows marketers to become publishers – build their audiences, and attract their own attention. While rented attention can be effective when you own your attention by creating content, you benefit in three major ways:

1. **You build awareness for your brand**

Your audience can't buy from you if they can't find you – and up to 93% of buying cycles start with a search online. Traditional advertising and outbound marketing can be an effective way of building awareness, but content marketing allows you to build organic awareness.

When your valuable content ranks highly on search engines or is shared widely on social networks, that's "free" brand awareness. And because your content will only rate highly or be shared when it's relevant, your audience will be less inclined to tune it out.

2. You create preference for your brand

Once you've established awareness, you need to develop a preference. Engaging content marketing creates preference through thought leadership it makes you a trusted source of information and education.

You can also create preference through relationships, which are strengthened whenever your content entertains or helps your buyers. All other things being equal, people are more likely to buy from companies with whom they have relationships. Of course, this requires you to create content that people like or even love.

3. You reach more buyers and customers, at lower costs

According to Forrester research, today's customers distrust and resent marketing that interrupts or intercepts them. Engaging content marketing is part of a natural conversation with current and potential customers, is relevant to their interests and behaviours, and builds a continuous story over time. Unlike traditional marketing, content pays dividends for a very long time, and this effect multiplies as you create more and more content. Note that this means that content marketing is not a short-term strategy – results will be small at first but will grow over time.

"Content builds relationships. Relationships are built on trust. Trust drives revenue."

- Andrew Davis

CONTENT MARKETING STRATEGY

Putting together a successful content marketing strategy will depend on the resources you have on hand. You'll want to determine which types of content are going to be the most relevant and effective to connect to your target audience. Additionally, you'll also want to pinpoint the ideal publishing platforms and social media sites to market and promote your content. All strategies for marketing content are unique, so you'll need to get creative as to how you approach the strategy for your business.

"Be so good they can't ignore you."

Steve Martin

The purpose of a content marketing strategy is to drive traffic and thus increase sales using that content. However, a solid strategy in content marketing for startups won't just increase profits, and it will increase brand awareness, as well as boosting user engagement. The content should whip up momentum in a sales funnel that gathers in new customers while keeping and nurturing the existing ones.

Steps to preparing a great content marketing strategy for your startup.

Developing a solid content marketing strategy will increase transparency and authority.Otherwise, you can waste a significant amount of time and money. The significance of content marketing has reached a higher position and has led to the growth of companies providing unique and appealing content. Entrepreneurs realise the importance of content marketing strategy in order to stay at a top position. People surfing the web will ignore low-quality content. A piece of content must serve the purpose of its creation.

Required outcome of the business

The required outcome of the business should clearly define what the business wishes to achieve, what are the key elements, what are the resources available and what is the overall mission. It is very important to define the role of content marketing and inbound marketing as a significant aspect.

Define your audience

What type of people make up your target audience? Most businesses have an idea of who their primary target is, so this should be a straightforward step- but if you aren't quite sure, then check out your competition. Find out who they are targeting, how they're doing it and the type of content that their audiences seem to enjoy.

Create content your target audience craves

While there are plenty of audiences that prefer videos, there are some that don't. Some prefer to read masses of text, and others simply don't. If you aren't sure what your audience prefers, then check out the competition. Videos do have a high conversion rate, higher than any other content type, so even if you operate in the mostly text, there is always room for a video or two.

Set goals

The idea of using content marketing is to boost sales through creating awareness, engaging readers, improving loyalty and building relationships. Hence, aggressive promotions throughout will not help. Rather than a general goal, break up your content marketing strategy into smaller, specific and realistic goals.

SMART

Specific
Measurable
Attainable
Relevant
Timely

If you're familiar with the term SMART, then use it. This is where many content marketing strategies go wrong.The basis of SMART- Specific, Measurable, Attainable, Relevant and Timely. There is nothing wrong with setting yourself challenging goals. However, you must remain realistic to deliver. What do you want to achieve? If you want to double your sales using content or add a thousand subscribers to your blog- that forms part of your strategy. In fact, you could say goals breathe life into the strategy- because they are the tools with which you measure your progress, and compare results.

Plan content

You've heard the saying

"If You Fail To Plan Then You Plan To Fail"

This is very apt when it comes to content marketing

When it comes to content marketing and branding ideas: you must plan. Review the objectives that you have put into your strategy and from that create a planning chart. So, what type of content is to be published? When is it to be published, and how often? Where will it be posted? Who will write the content, and what topics should be covered?

Marketing and promotion

Hitting "publish" doesn't equal reads. Make sure you get your content in front of your target audience- whether that means you pay for adverts, use SEO, social media or influencer marketing. Branding your content marketing give a visual identity and puts your business in the minds of others, so do this consistently.

Monitor and adapt

Monitor your progress regularly. If things aren't moving as planned, or you aren't meeting goals then tweak your strategy.

Track and measure

With your content marketing strategy up and running for a while, you need to track performance. Thus, the first thing to do is implement trackable strategies. Track the right metrics depending on your objectives. Some of the metrics you can measure include:

- The page views and documents accumulated
- The number of social media shares
- The social networks that bring the most traffic
- The number of consumers you have managed to convert into leads and actual sales

You can always change or delete content that is not aligned with your content marketing objectives.

Proper analysis

Business analysis must tell the exact position of business, its customer base, buying potential, products, and services, and failures, in any. Without any proper analysis, it is not possible to define an organisation's capability. Creation of successful content management plan depends on the organization's current status in the market.

Marketing objectives

Some short to medium term objectives must be set to achieve the target. The content management strategy should be able to achieve every objective and required outcomes. It should deliver focus, timescales and appropriate content. It should emphasise on growing the reputation of business. Marketing done through content should have a positive output and strong voice.

Feedback and comments

Encourage potential customers and site visitors to leave feedback and comments. Devote more time to incorporate the changes as a part of your business's content marketing strategy. After making the changes, let the visitors know that you appreciated the feedback and made the required changes in the content.

Content developing is the first step towards an effective marketing strategy. You will increase transparency and authority, as well as a trust by providing quality content. A brief note from organisational experts communicating the beneficial features of their products and services is termed as a good piece of content. Audience widely appreciates the quality content, and you will be able to get desired results as a part of content marketing strategy.

"Brands need to take the phrase 'acting like a publisher' literally."

- Dietrich Mateschitz

WHY DO YOU NEED A CONTENT MARKETING STRATEGY

Content marketing is more than just a popular buzzword in the Internet marketing industry. The concept of content marketing underscores a powerful technique to promote a business on the Internet. By creating great content (such as a video, article, or infographic) and marketing that content (via Facebook and Google+, etc.) your business can take advantage of many opportunities to connect with potential customers.

The methods behind content marketing offer limitless channels to exploit your ideas. In short, you can create content in various forms and distribute it many different ways. And just as limitless as the channels to market your content are the potential benefits for your business.

All types of companies can improve their marketing efforts by producing and sharing awesome content. In fact, marketing software provider Kapost has found through its research that per dollar, content marketing contributes up to to three times more leads that traditional online advertising, such as paid search. For this reason, creating a content marketing strategy can be a momentous game-changer for your business.

"Think of it more as publishing instead of marketing. Be authentic as a publisher and create content that helps you connect to everyone else...because they're already connected."

Mitch Joel

How will content marketing help your business?

If you are wondering if you really have a need for a content marketing strategy for you business, the answer to that question is a resounding yes. However, it is important for you to understand that your content marketing strategy (for a small business) will be different from the content marketing strategy of a large business. Content marketing will attract attention to the point where you will be able actually to build relationships with those people. Your content marketing will help you to accomplish several things, including establishing yourself as a subject matter expert and building trust, credibility and trustworthiness.

Although content marketing offers a tonne of advantages, there are three main advantages that your business can realise:

- Build Brand Awareness
- Inbound Traffic to Your Site
- Generate Natural Link Popularity for SEO

Building Brand Awareness

As the foundation to marketing your content on the web, building brand awareness is further enhanced when the audience is engaged.This audience engagement is what fuels respect for your brand and bolsters a potential relationship. As a result, the quality and relevancy of your content are paramount. Any content you publish is a reflection of your business and its brand, so you'll want to be creative and use the right context that relates to your target audience.

Some of the highest levels of audience engagement derive from visually-based content. Videos are a powerful medium to communicate to a potentially massive audience. And by optimising videos for better search engine exposure (also known as search engine optimisation or "SEO"), the overall marketing potential skyrockets.Also effective in the visual content category are images, infographics, cartoons and comics. Exercise your creativity and produce a compelling form of content that can help build awareness in your brand.

“The only way to win at content marketing is for the reader to say, ‘This was written specially for you’.”

JamieTurner

Inbounding Traffic to Your Site

The cornerstone of content marketing is to inbound traffic to your site. Marketing your content is a very powerful way to promote your niche or unique selling proposition. As long as you present the right calls to action, the individuals that interact with your content will be more likely to visit your website.

This form of traffic is unique because of the prior interaction that users experience with your content. The best ways to inbound quality traffic to your site is use your content to inform and educate your target audience. Addressing relevant issues, questions, and concerns is a good way to achieve this. For example, a criminal defense lawyer may benefit from publishing an article about 'what to do when faced with Drink Driving charges.'

Generating Natural Link Popularity for SEO

When content goes viral, it tends to attract a lot of social attention. People usually link to popular content (link popularity,) and as a result, the content can earn a high level of authority. From an SEO standpoint, if a web page has a high level of authority, then the outbound links coming from that page will be more powerful. This concept of SEO (commonly referred to as "link bait") is one of the many useful approaches to content marketing.

Think of your wonderful piece of content as link bait for your SEO efforts. In almost any form of content, whether a video, article, or graphic, you can typically include a link that directs back to your site. For instance, graphics and videos will usually always have supportive text or an author attribution. Here you can include a bit about who you are, as well as a link back to your website. If your content generates a lot of buzzes and people start linking to it, the SEO value of your content will only become more powerful.

DEVELOPING CONTENT CREATION

Content creation is the backbone of any online business with intentions of establishing a long lasting presence. Equally important to creating content is the ability to efficiently circulate it around on the internet. Being that content development can be labor intensive it is important to establish a time efficient and effective strategy for its distribution. Even better would be to develop a means in which the creation and distribution functions were seamlessly integrated. In doing so, you would be able to make better use of this online marketing strategy in a more time efficient manner.

Content Types

Text

When addressing a target audience with a direct message, it's the written word that remains a favourite option. Articles which utilize the language, expressions, terms and words unique to a particular industry, niche or market automatically set the context and tone of the message. With this kind of content, impeccable grammar is the highest priority, followed closely in importance by the proper structuring of sentences and paragraphs in order to command audience attention and send clear messages.

Images

Photos, diagrams, infographics and computer-generated graphics attract the human eye and help to deliver a message by illustrating an organization's products, services, concepts and ideas. Such image content must be high quality in design, composition, colour and clarity.

Videos

The ever popular use of video on the Internet serves a variety of purposes from providing product or procedural demonstrations, to giving a face to either a business or product, to teaching classes halfway around the world to generating a buzz in social networking platforms.

Infographics

Images accompanied by small amounts of text referred to as infographics are the latest Internet and media craze. Infographics are an increasingly popular, visual way to relay information, data and sometimes complex concepts and messages. Conveniently eliminating the obvious sales pitch, infographics can be utilized to effectively share a company's story in a creative and entertaining way.

Standard original content can also be leveraged into other forms of content like

- Microsites
- White papers

- Webinars or webcasts
- Branded content tools
- Research reports
- Traditional media
- Print magazines
- Digital magazines
- Mobile content
- Podcasts
- eBooks
- Print newsletters

Different Aspects to Consider on Content Creation

There is a whole lot more to content creation than simply writing, as we are about to explain in this book.

Why is content creation so important?

There has been a recent shift in strategy by major organizations and corporations, from producing cost efficient content to high quality and marketable content. As many businesses have discovered and continue to discover, the content creation process can be used to increase website traffic and brand awareness, as well as search engine optimization for their website. These are a number of key areas, as viral and internet marketing becomes increasingly bigger and more potent than ever before.

First Things First: Creating a Headline

The advice around creating the best headlines depends almost entirely on what your business is and consequently who your target market is going to be. You also need to take into account which platform you are publishing your content on, as this can change your strategy dramatically. A couple of the general rules around headlines is to keep them as short as possible, while also using keywords when it is appropriate and plausible.

Knowing the audience that you are trying to target is integral to writing an engaging headline, so ensuring that you do your research on this aspect is a key area for content creation as if no one is enticed to click on it, then who will read it?

Developing new content

The key to having a successful content creation strategy is ensuring that you are developing new and unique content on a regular basis.Much of this depends on the type of content that you are hoping to develop, whether it is an opinion piece, informational, research-based, or other type.

One feature to also keep an eye on is to add a call to action, wherever it is appropriate. For example, if you are a plumbing company and are writing an article on how to spot potential plumbing problems, then you may want to follow this up at the bottom of the article with a call to action for contacting you if they have any of the issues listed.

How to make your content effective

One method you can use to ensure that your content is effective is by using language that is relevant to the audience as if the intended audience is not necessarily well versed in a certain area then bombarding them with technical terms and other information is a sure way to lose them as a reader.

Content creation should be about educating and informing the reader, while also posing questions and answering them. By combining all of the above elements listed and implementing them into your content creation strategy, you will soon reap the rewards of your valuable content.

Excellent tools that can be used for both creating content and distributing it more efficiently online.

Social Network Sites

Social network sites such as Twitter are an excellent source of news and information for content development. Also sites like these can also be used as a part of your content distribution strategy by simply posting your work on the site for other members to view and share as well.

Blog(s)

Having a blog of your own is a great platform to showcase your content for visitors to view. By visiting other blogs, you can pick up new information or ideas which you can then develop your own unique content for use in the future. When using content for marketing purposes online, it is always wise to have your own blog to make the best use of your efforts.

Social Bookmark Sites

Social bookmark sites such as Digg, Delicious or Stumbleupon just to name a few are great sources of new content. On the flip side sites like these are also terrific platforms for content distribution purposes as well. Simply bookmarking your own content and having it circulated one of these sites can tremendously boost your exposure.

Article Directories

Submitting articles online is one of the most efficient ways to saturate the internet with content you have created. When directories publish your articles other businesses and publishers, using content much in the same way as you, are then allowed use your article provided you are credited as the author. These directories are also a great source of information for your own content development purposes as well.

Forums

Forums are very easy to locate on any topic and are a great source of targeted information as well as effective distribution points for your content. Out of the 5 different online locations mentioned here, forums are perhaps the most targeted for your content in terms of developing and distributing. Content creation is the starting point of a very effective online marketing strategy that also requires a means for distributing it on the internet.

The effectiveness of written content creation, in particular, will depend upon the right strategy being used regardless of whether the business is an online one, or a bricks and mortar type.

The benefits of using content creation tools

If you are still using basic tools, such as Microsoft Word, for every piece of content that you create, then this article is for you, as we describe the benefits of the different content creation tools that are available.

While there is nothing wrong with Microsoft Word for document creation, the chances are that there is a set of content creation tools that can streamline your process, while also opening up a whole new world of functionality.

XML Structured Authoring

If you are not familiar with XML structured authoring, then it is worth giving a brief description as it is central to most content creation tools that you are likely to use. Where basic Word processing programs can be configured by eye to match the layout that is desired, XML authoring allows more advanced publishing software that separate the content from the formatting.

Separate Formatting and Content

In this respect, it is a little like HTML, where a code such as would be used to give a predefined format to the text, such as 12 pt. Times New Roman bold text, as an example. Using these tools allow for a much easier and less time-intensive way of recreating similar designs and themes over numerous different types of content and documents.

Cross Platform Publishing

A really nifty feature of most XML content creation tools is being able to automatically change the format to suit the platform it is going to be published on. If we take our example from earlier, and say that on the web the formatted text would come out as a 12 Pt. Times New Roman bold text, we may want it to change to 14 pt. Italic Arial font for when it is displayed on the phone, for example.

This versatility in these tools ensures that managing and publishing content is much quicker and easier, as the author does not have the manual task of reformatting and designing for each platform.

Reusing Content

Another benefit of using XML content creation is the ability to reuse components and content, instead of rewriting, or copying and pasting that information from elsewhere. By pointing to the source of the component, or content, it allows several documents to use one source of information.

The main benefit of this is that, if this component needs to be updated, only the one source of information is required to be amended, as it will automatically update the other sheets, making it far more accurate and streamlined.

Purpose of content creation

- Information is the core of content creation - about what an organisation wants to share with its market and potential customers. Through information sharing businesses can increase brand awareness, boost their customer bases and develop and maintain positive relationships with their existing clients. Content can also be leveraged for other objectives, including:
- The engagement of employees via company blogs
- Easy recruiting through organisation web pages which are highly representative of the company's vision, direction, and goals
- Greater business development, especially when such content is shared between businesses (BUSINESS 2 BUSINESS)

Keys to successful content creation

Identify The Audience: To send an appropriate and effective message a business must correctly identify the audience with whom it is delivering the information.

Style Guide

To develop a business' overall brand and ensure the same message is being delivered through each method and channel being utilised, content consistency is critical. To ensure the coherence of a message, style elements must be decided upon before the creation process begins. Such elements include tone of voice, words to be used and choice of language.

New Content

Just like produce sold in a market, online content must be fresh if it is to attract the attention of the target audience and encourage them to return for more relevant information in the future. Unique content also needs to be insightful so that it provides information that readers will find useful and want to learn more about. In this age of information, content is not just about what the business wants to relay, but rather, what the audience or searchers want or need.

As a marketing tool, content must convey the value of the business, its services and products, along with the business' niche authority, to the targeted consumer in a way that's informative. Once convinced of the business' value, the audience will find the next step of following a call to action to feel much more natural.

Ongoing Development

While consumer behaviour undergoes changes, so does market conditions that can also be accompanied by new challenges and increases in the competition. This requires the creation of new content to keep the consumer informed. Those who create this type of content should also undertake continuous learning by researching quality sources of authoritative information to be used in the new content. This self-education results in new approaches and aspects to write about while offering a way to build on previously acquired information, allowing the content creator to enhance their authority and credibility with the audience.

Reusing Content

With imagination, creativity and resourcefulness, old content can have new life breathed into it. Repurposing or reusing content can come in the form of images being converted into slide show presentations, video clips can be arranged as part of a webinar series, and text entries can be incorporated into newsletters and eMagazines.

Ideally, the responsibility of content creation should only be assigned to a team or person who either has an understanding of your industry and establishment or who can conduct the necessary research to learn about it. This understanding will be manifested in the way the material is written, revealing the creator's comprehension of your services' or products' unique strengths, selling points and current market trends.

While many large organizations provide their clients content creation services through an in-house development team, it's important to remember that aside from adequate service/product knowledge and writing skills, such staff members must also have a solid grasp of best practices regarding SEO (search engine optimization). Perhaps more importantly, they need to be motivated to expend the time that is required to stay up to date with changing trends in premium content creation.
Whether you have your own content writing staff or you commission a content writing service, it's critical that they have full comprehension of the special strategies that need to be used in the online business world.

What to Expect in the Content Creation Process

There are a lot more to content creation than you think. That is why it is important to have a team of content experts behind you when you decide to start focusing on creating high-value content. After all, content is how your company communicates, both internally and externally, and you want to make sure that the right points are being communicated in a professional manner.

In this book, we are going to look at what it involved in content creation and also how you can benefit by outsourcing your content creation to a firm that specialises in content. By doing this, you will have the experts as mentioned above to help you define a strategy, as well as implement the latest content-related technology to make creating and managing your content much easier.

Planning and Strategizing

Content creation must involve a plan, or strategy if you want the content to be successful. Work with specialists to draw up a strategy that will offer you a timeline of content production, how it will be delivered and managed and also what will happen afterwards. This can be done through meetings and workshops with your firm and the specialists so that you can ensure that everything that you need to achieve with your content is covered. They can also keep you in the loop on what is going on in relation to content creation and best practices. You can imagine related goals for your business and the content experts will strategize on how to achieve them.

Content Management

Before you start on content creation, you need to have a content management system in place. This will ensure that the content is stored, organised, published and governed in a way that everybody agrees upon and in a way that simplifies content creation. Without management, creation and storage can be completely disorganised, and your content quality will not be consistent. When drawing up a content strategy, it is always a good idea to develop a management plan too, so that content creation can begin as soon as possible and be a smooth process.

Content Authoring

After drawing up a plan and figuring out how content management will be done, it is time to start with content authoring. It is often best to have your high-value authoring done by a team of professional writers. You can work with them and tell them the most important points that you want to see in the content and make as many edits as you like, but it is best to leave the professional writers to the writing to ensure clarity and good structure.

CONTENT MARKETING FUNNEL

The Content Marketing Funnel is a method of using tailor-made content to optimise the conversion of leads into paying customers. The method involves targeting points with different types of content throughout the buying decision process, depending on which stage of the process they are currently in. The idea of the funnel is relatively new and has emerged largely due to the increase in global interconnectivity in recent years and the variety of different types of content available to the marketing industry as a result.

Marketers are now able to support sales in an unprecedented way by targeting each part of the funnel with unique, stage-specific content types that help qualify, nurture, and convert leads into paying customers. Strategic use of content opens up a world of opportunities.

The purpose of the funnel is to convert as many leads as possible into actual customers who are willing to pay for your products or services.

Content marketing for the business 2 business marketing funnel

A typical business 2 business decision involves getting buy ins from multiple stakeholders, market research, vendor comparison, credentials validation, negotiation and budget planning. This makes it important for business 2 business marketers to adopt a more strategic approach for long term success. Although "close it in the first shot" kind of tactical approach works for short term success successful business 2 business marketers are the one's who help prospects in their decision making at various stages of their buying cycle.
Business 2 business Marketing Funnel

A typical business 2 business marketing funnel has five stages

Awareness
At this stage, the prospect is looking to find out what exactly his problem is and how he can solve it. It is important for your brand to be discoverable during this stage as you get into the user's mind earlier than the competition. A prospect is looking for a thought leader in the industry to guide him to a DIY solution or a vendor who can help him.

What to write about: To capture the attention of the user as a business 2 business brand, you have to provide information on your blogs and social channels about latest trends, benchmarks, recent surveys and expert insights. Providing this type of content positions you as a thought leader in the industry.

Consideration

During this stage the user enquires more about your company and service. He is trying to understand how your offerings can fulfill his need. Prospects at this stage are looking at all the services you offer, product features, your pricing structure and investigating on any pitfalls or missed out use cases.

What to write about: Writing content on how the solution you provide fits in with different technologies or how your offering can address various use cases a prospect might have will win your prospect's interest.

Comparison

During this stage, the prospect is evaluating between multiple players in your industry. Various factors like price, past success, online reviews, features, support and reputation are weighed against before choosing a vendor.A successful business 2 business marketer can influence this aspect of the funnel by understanding context and user research patterns. You can bid on your competitions keywords and direct them to a landing page which proves why you are better. Shopify does this remarkably well.

Conversion

Your prospect needs a final push before hitting the pay button. During this phase, you have to answer this fundamental fear "Why should I trust you? How well, you respond to this question determines who closes the deal. You or your competition.

What to write about when planning your content marketing plan: Past success stories, ROI to expect, answered FAQs, what to expect when they work with you, your methodology and values, your credentials and market reputation.

Retention

This is one of the most important sectors because gaining customers is expensive and hard work and you are much better retaining the clients that you have rather than having a high churn rate. What converts a user is NOT what helps them stick. Once a prospect is your customer product/service support is critical. Without customer support, churn rates take a hit, and a lost customer can be bad for the reputation of the company as well as expensive to replace. At the same time, a customer happy can be a brand advocate bringing in more loyal users of your product or service along with the ongoing revenue from them.

What to write about: As a business 2 business content marketer, it is important that enough support is provided to your existing customer base in the form of video/PDF tutorials, case studies and guides. Detailed guides can help fight user frustration and eliminate elaborate discussion on the phone by your customer support teams.

As a business 2 business content marketer, it is important to address content which fits with all stages of the buying cycle. Long term thinking, patience and strategic approach will lead to sustainable success and contribute to organic business growth.

25348703R00028

Printed in Great Britain
by Amazon